ARACHNIDS ANONYMOUS AND OTHER POEMS

PRAKASH RAGHUPATHI

Made with ❤ on the Notion Press Platform
www.notionpress.com

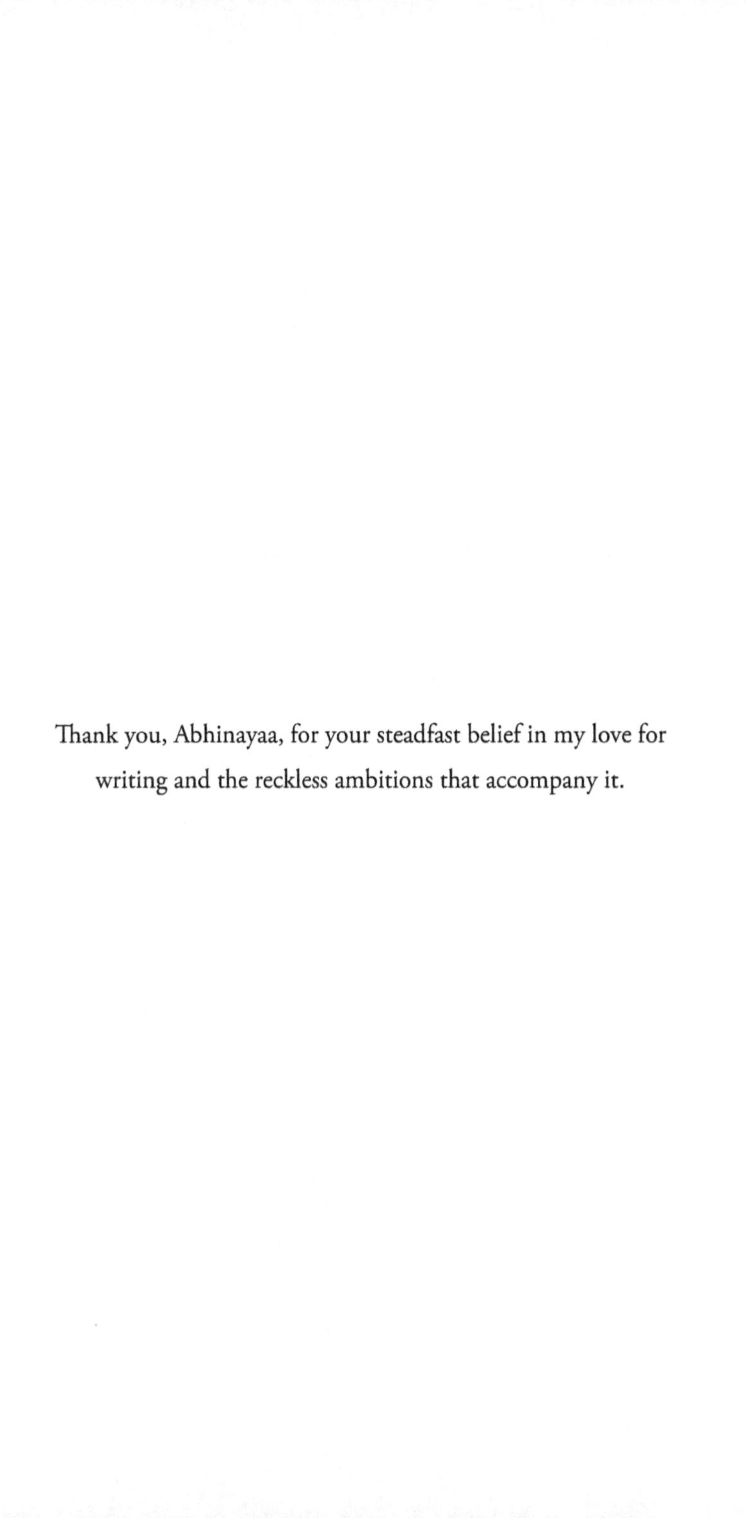

Thank you, Abhinayaa, for your steadfast belief in my love for writing and the reckless ambitions that accompany it.

Contents

Contents

Foreword

None of these poems is AI generated.

None of **my poems** will ever be.

Preface

Thank you for purchasing one copy of my book. If you've bought two copies or encouraged someone to buy one copy, let me tell you that it means a lot to me. If you've bought one copy and encouraged two others to buy one copy each, let me tell you, I didn't expect this book to be a bestseller. If you live outside of India and you purchased the book, or you asked someone living abroad to buy the book, let me tell you, I didn't expect it to cross borders. If you gifted someone a copy of this book, let me tell you, it has spiders. But I hope the person you gave this book to doesn't let it die an unread death in the cobwebs.

Acknowledgements

Thank you for buying the book. How are you doing? I hope you enjoy the read. You can DM and tell me how you liked it. You can reach for the stars on Amazon and Flipkart, too, if you want. No pressure. Four stars would do.

My Instagram handle is @prakashr2711.

Another Day, Another Dollar

What better way to start this book than talk about the grind that refuses to come to a grinding halt?

1. God Read This and Asked, 'You Talkin' to Me?'

If life is designed to take its course,

Why do we have free will?

If destiny holds the strings to Earthly drill,

Why do I pray my voice hoarse?

The Commandments, ten or more

Did man write them, or are they words of the divine?

Should I strive for peace and calm?

Should I resort to using the deadly Napalm?

So you say I got to pay my dues,

I got to balance my karma,

Playing to the niceties is part of my dharma,

But then I look at the basterds about town,

And wonder if these 'words of wisdom' are just a big ruse.

2. Horn. OK. Fuck it, please?

As I crawl through the serpentine, multi-colored brawl,
Alongside frowning brows that little joys cannot enthrall,
It's as if Murphy holds the strings, ready to pivot everything toward the wrong,
Nothing can drown the fury, the anger, the sorrow... not even a calming Dylan song.
As I pass through the calming blues, the ominous yellows, and the dreadful red,
I wonder, 'Why the fuck can't the Father just give me my Daily Bread?'
Why must I burn and burn and bear the brunt?
Why do I have to be the prey and not the predator out there to hunt?
'Life has its plan for you,' said the wise.
Those words made me want to hack and place him on ice.
Every comforting thought, word, and phrase is just an excuse,
I was born into this world to merely face God's abuse.

3. Monday Bruises

After a weekend of laidback sighs,
Memories blurred by spurious highs,
I feel pain in the middle of my chest,
It's not life-threatening, but it won't let me rest.
There's no wound, so I don't scream.
But it feels like a stab in the back.
There's no blood, just a big lump in my throat,
And so I'm unable to faint or even hit the sack.
How must I let go of this horrible feeling?
'Dive headfirst into it,' said a hustler.
'Let go and let things happen,' said a healer.
I tried everything and failed,
So finally, I just called my dealer.

4. A Famous Man Does Not Like This Poem

The unicorn said to me,
'Come with me, and I will take you to a new world.'
'Where is that,' I asked.
'A world where the population is sparse,
where the Western Ghats are green, year-round
and you're closer to the stars.'
'Am I rich in that world,' I asked.
'Limitless are the pleasures,
No proverbial clouds,
only silver linings.
And the real ones bring pleasant, mild showers,
And rainbows when the sun is shining!'
'Am I happy in that world' I asked.
'That's really up to you.' said the unicorn.

5. Red Neighborhood

You pick up a pen, a hammer, a shovel, or a tong,
The day is a drudge; you're trying to get through with some
help from your favourite song.
Turning passion into misery and misery into passion,
You confuse and complain but never give up because 'That's
not in fashion,'
White-collar, blue-collar, collarless on Fridays.
'Dress to kill' and dressed to die,
In the hope of just a little praise.
But remember, comrade, without you, they aren't worth a
dime
And standing up for your rights has never been and will never
be a crime.
So the next time some snoot comes and interrupts your
favourite song,
Don't forget; you wield dangerous power —
You're holding a pen, a hammer, a shovel, or a tong.

6. Happy Ending

Revisit the sepia-tinged memories
of your worst nightmares,
and they will always make you laugh.

My Wife Asked Me To Write A Few Happy Poems

Here's why I can't...

7. Thirty Years Later

It took me the blink of an eye,
To go from toddler to teen,
To join the rebellion,
And think every moment is a movie scene.
It took me a breath,
To turn 20-something,
To think I'd arrived,
And always 'go all in or nothing.'
But it's taken many lifetimes,
To turn thirty,
To not leap into the unknown,
To not burn it all down with flaming Bourbon.
I'd give anything to turn back the clock,
To the time when Dwayne Johnson was still just 'The Rock.'
I'd want it back every single day,
But I'll tell myself that it's better this way.

But honestly, here's better…
You're still out cold,
But you have money to buy a sweater.

8. You Are Wrong. Am I Right?

The biting sermons of a grandfather
Resurface decades later -
They happen when the muscles get sore,
When life starts treating you
Like you're an uninhibited whore.

Amidst the stampede of thoughts,
A familiar voice echoes,
It's happy, gruff, can't help being sarcastic -
'Had you listened to me, there would be no woe.'

'First, work on yourself,' he would say -
'That's the easiest way to get by,
Stay grounded, bow down,
Only the birds are meant to fly.'

It's the system that's broken, (Grandpa)
'But first, you must work on yourself.'

Freedom is an expired token,
'But first, you must work on yourself.'

It's the society that's deranged,
'But first, you must work on yourself.'

The government has my noose arranged,
'But first, you must work on yourself.'

It's the laws that are bent,
'But first, you must work on yourself.'
A life of bondage is a life well spent?
'Don't overthink... first, work on yourself.'

9. Gendarmerie

There's a hard knock on the door,
It's the gendarmerie.
Stay quiet, don't cause an uproar,
It's the brutal gendarmerie.
They wield weapons,
'The plain-clothed? They are gendarmerie?'
Yes, They are here to kill,
The self-anointed gendarmerie.

10. (K)inktober

We live in a world that creates in October,
And destroys the purpose
through the next eleven —
Allows verse to flow free
and become a meme.
Killing the very purpose of ink
and every life
that is supposed to be a dream.

11. ____pur

Genocides beyond compare,
W. H. Davies, all we (can) do is stand and stare.
Fill in the blanks.
Point Blank.
Humanity beware.

12. LSP is a Schedule 1 Drug

If only lemon and salt
were just **lemon and salt!**
If only a pumpkin could be a pumpkin,
And not a counter eye to my ever-so-jealous kin.

13. Old Monk at Large

Are you love?

Or am I just reciprocating?

Are you happiness?

Or a weakness debilitating?

Are you my messiah?

Or am I insinuating?

Are you my saviour?

Or am I merely hallucinating?

14. Meditorial

Thinking about the oil crisis,
about the putrid vices.
Thinking about elephants
and the masters of disguise — those bloody sycophants!
Thinking about the flood
and the revolution that ended a dud.
Couldn't muster the courage to read myself some Freud.
Thinking about it all
while listening to some timeless Pink Floyd.

15. That's a Good Question.

'When the locust take over the world,
Know that you are no longer on top of the food chain.'
Can we get back on top?
'Are you ready to get off the high horse and stay grounded?'

16. Mooncalf

'I see an angry face,' I said.
'The moon reflects your nature,' said my father.
I spent the next 35 years,
Imagining what other people see in the moon,
The face winks at me, now.

17. Who's Your Hibiscus?

A ferocious shade of orange,
Overshadows the all-seasonals -
The pink, white, and red
Can do little to overcome its presence,
To them, even nature is biased,
Capable of committing calculated treason.

Arachnids Anonymous

This is what you are here for, aren't you?

18. 'Hi, I am Tony Tarantula. I ate my friend Gary Grasshopper.'

What could I have done —
'Nature takes its course,'
My father used to say until his voice turned hoarse.
'We are creatures of the night —
the moon is our guiding light,
And He said we must do what it takes to satiate our appetite.'
Sometimes, I feel I should've been bred in captivity —
Feeding on what's fed, fed more, perhaps, during a festivity.
The Earth shook that day, and it wasn't the crickets… I knew.
My legs trembled… was it the demon again? Chasing mildew?
My father used to say that — 'Demons roam about at night,
Don't worry, my son; he's a friend — he does what needs to be done,
He hath said there is no wrong, there is no right.'
So, as I said, the Earth shook that day, and it wasn't the crickets… I knew.
As my legs kicked back, it felt alien… it felt like it was somebody new.
Sometimes, I feel I should've died young —

Avoided this absurdity; defied the putrid prophecies of Carl
Jung.
So, like I said, it felt alien… it felt like it was somebody new,
I prayed, 'Let it be the godforsaken frog. Not my friends; I
had only a few.'
'Suck it up, son,' my father used to say,
'He who hath the venom has the final word!'
'Don't be one of them, son. Don't be one of those with their
souls all stirred.'
So, like I said, I prayed, 'Let it be the godforsaken frog. Not
my friends; I had only a few.'
Sadly, it was someone I dearly knew.
Why couldn't I see before it was all done?
He lay there… suffering, waiting for the pain to come
undone.
What could I have done — I had to ease the pain.
'Rest in peace, Gary! You will avenge yourself as a bird or the
torrential rain.'
I mourn to this day for my green friend… now estranged,
And wish I knew my father… was one of those deranged.

19. 'They used to call me Big Boy.'

'How blessed am I?' - at least, I thought I was,

Wandering in search of love,

Up and about, in keeping with Nature's laws.

Just a few feet away from New South Wales,

There was a bushland I'd like to call home and heaven,

Where I hoped to find my soulmate until —

'The attractive ones are in suburbia,' said my dear mate

Davon.

And so I took to the streets,

Filled with people, smoke, and smells so rotten,

Wondering how cursed human life could be,

Wondering if they'd read Hardin's 'Tragedy of the Commons.'

Nevertheless, it felt nice for a while — I met a few suitable

matches,

I had a good time with them — survived with no wounds,

just a few scratches.

Little did I know what humans were born to do,

Little did I know how venomous they were,

Until I slipped into a shoe.

It was just after the summer rain,

The sun was out and about,

I just needed some shade,

And so I detour-ed from my earlier route.

The next thing I knew, I was confined to a box,

Accused of a crime like Amanda Knox.

I was to stand trial for a crime I didn't commit,

'It's my instinct,' I said —

A defense the prosecutors chose to conveniently omit.

'Big Boy' — a repulsive christening in front of a crowd —

Equally repulsive, disgusting, and oh so proud.

Contrary to their belief, it was a repulsive, disgusting jail.

Uncontrolled, angered, I dove straight for her fingernail.

Before she could gasp and the rest of the vermins could grasp,

I scampered as fast as I could,

Found my way back to the bushland —

A place I left, never again I would!

It haunts me even today — I didn't intend to kill.

Maybe it was the price they had to pay… maybe it was Nature's will?

20. Itsy Bitsy Spider

Why would I ever climb up the waterspout?!
Did they think I was so naive,
And why would I stay till the rain washed me out?!
Why would I commit a folly so grave?
Ever since I was born,
people be writing me off —
As a teeny, tiny, itsy, bitsy being.
When I told them angrily, 'I ain't,'
They would shrug and unapologetically scoff.
Wherever I went,
I was the simpleton face of a silly rhyme As if I was always on
Prozac;
My life was all hay and endless sunshine.
Little did they know,
I, too, could be strong and brawley,
I wasn't just cutesy like the ilk,
Born out of Walt's famous folly.

21. Snow White and the Vegetarian Huntsman

'I'd like a salad, I said,
She looked at me
Like I'd eaten her alive.
I was a creature that could change,
I am not Robert Clive.
Why must I always be hunting lizards,
They are creepy; their tails grow back!
I like my veggies, and I am good with that,
She should've just got them… stuck to her track.
She pretended as if she knew me in and out,
In her pretty outfit and her face all pale,
So what if I don't like Blue Label or a beer,
I get inebriated with just a ginger ale.
Why must she judge me,
And ask me why I walk so fast,
One day I couldn't take it anymore,
'You get your tip. So cut the crap!'
She got all worked up,
More worked up than my vegetarian appetite,
Sometimes I wish the dwarves had killed her,
Before she became all proud and full of spite.
I don't like frogs, insects, or any of them arthropods,

I find them disgusting,
As disgusting as that fairy tale broad.

22. The Recluse

I love an evening to myself,

With no else to fiddle with my back,

Have a drink, listen to Vivaldi,

Yawn, like no one's watching,

And just hit the sack.

What's this pressure, I ask?

The pressure to literally 'hang out'

Spinning webs of gossip and drunken angst,

And intellectualize things that no one cares about —

Why must I visit the Northern Lights,

'Oooo! It's just bananas."

I am happy being around Kentucky and Illinois,

Damn! I even visited a brother in Indiana.

I love a day to myself,

Sometimes writing, learning words like 'schisms',

Or just sit back gurgling something necrotic,

And binging on 'Curb Your Enthusiasm'

23. Banana Republic

In our prefecture,

It's a sin to say anything out loud,

But one thing we are allowed to say,

Is 'Two's company, three's a crowd'.

You see when there are just two,

It's more like a discussion,

When there are three or more,

There are going to be tears, bullets, and concussions.

I wonder why most can't just stay put,

Why must they yell and scream and shout,

Do they not know the price they have to pay?

They'll all be slaughtered like an innocent cow.

There's no room for protest or hate here,

Not even an emotion like L-mao

24. It's Not All Rosy in the Garden

I'm an artisan who weaves orb webs,

I've been known for my craft,

For eons, through floods and peaceful ebbs.

I live a life of color — at least, I thought I did,

Until I saw what I saw — it was dark and sordid.

I always believed that crime, once punished,

Would never see the light of the day or the dark of a night,

History does repeat itself, I know…

But no one wants another Fred West or John Dwight?!

Life was good for long in the green,

Elizabeth wrote, 'Eat. Prey. Love.' here, did you know?

Who knew among the lilies and the plums,

A heinous figure would come to grow?!

He was lured to the blood like a Pavlovian dog to a bell,

He sure was in cahoots with the Devil,

The place was indeed scary as Hell.

I still see him from time to time,

Walking into the garden with a sack on his back,

Wishing his victims were born as spiders —

united in the ultimate payback.

25. The Black Widow Sestin-aah!

In the river that runs next door,

I saw her quivering reflection.

Silhouetted, hourglassed, and a distinctive mark in red.

'Is it the famed widow,' I thought.

After all, it was late spring,

And she would be looking for a mate.

What does she look for in a mate?

What would it take for her to let me through her door?

Would this be my time — my proverbial spring?

Maybe I should crawl to the river and see my reflection…

'Am I worth her,' I thought

To be with her and then fade away in blood red?

I've lost many brothers to this Voluptas, clad in red,

Each of them lost their drive to live to the passion to mate,

'Is it my time to be part of that legacy,' I thought.

Is it my turn to be greeted by the Keeper of Keys at the Door?

I saw her shift in that somewhat monochrome reflection,

Even the happiest of flowers shudder when she does that in

the spring.

A season where all good things must thrive… it is the spring!

Why must she color the yellows and blues and green in

Lucifer's red?

So much so, even the water shivered in the river bearing her reflection…

Ebbing away, thinking, 'Why must she have this murderous desire to mate?

Can't the maker show her the Darwinian exit door?'

'I wouldn't want her to,' I thought.

'I want her, and I want her for myself,' I thought.

All through summer, the fall, and every spring.

I'd let her have her way… I'd willingly hold open the door,

From the yellow of dawn to when the sky is red.

She can have them… have them all for a mate,

I'd bow to her even if she doesn't care… I'd quench my thirst with her reflection.

The quivering reflection broke my passionate dream.

'Where did she go,' I thought.

Had the hunt begun… the hunt to find her mate?

Had she devoured her passion for this spring?

Had I lost my chance to be the eternal bearer of her red?

And then I saw her… right outside my door.

I was her choice… her marked prey for this spring,

It was a night of passion… replete with all I wanted in red!

And…

26. I am Daddy-Longlegs

I've always agreed with Žižek —

'Humanity is okay. But 99% of people are boring idiots.'

I've crawled up the walls of many;

All they do is couch and grouch,

Or sit under the dim lights,

And endlessly debauch.

They'd spot me and stare,

Oooh and aah at my daddy-longlegs,

Destroy my home and hold me down by my legs,

Until they're satisfied or have emptied their kegs.

Dejected, insulted, stripped of my pride,

I boarded a ship that almost drowned in the high tide.

I was curious and furious —

I wanted to burn the bridge.

I wanted to learn how to make them suffer,

And I knew who could teach me; it was only Slavoj.

'What makes you depressed, he asked.

I didn't have an answer.

'It's watching stupid people be happy.'

That seemed as much to please me,

As a man's senses pleasured by a burlesque dancer.

Thank you, Slavoj,

I need revenge no more,

I don't need imprecations; no need to call them a whore.
I am content being who I am,
I won't let them get to me, those Earth's worthless dregs,
I am proud of who I am — I am fuckin daddy-longlegs.

Love

Bittersweet, isn't it?

27. Love is Like a Pint of Beer

First you get the froth,

It's all fun and frolic -

Fake mustaches,

The first contact with the lips,

Muscles all relaxed,

The mind at peace,

Makes you feel

you're cut from the same cloth.

Then, you get to the gold,

When you start to unravel beautiful stories untold,

The period can last long or short,

Depends on how patiently the pint you can hold.

There's flirtation, there's joy,

There's hope, there's trust,

There's lust and wanderlust.

There are dreams of a happy ever after,

Every passing moment brings even more laughter.

There's music, there's dance,

There are plans of a honeymoon in France.

And then you hit the bottom,

All flat, bitter, and hard to swallow,

When harsh truths come uncovered,

When words are about knots and have nots,
Where your heart is hollow,
And your love seems shallow,
No bubbles, no fizz, no courage,
Just an empty glass,
And many reasons to wallow.

Take it in slow, my friend,
It's an acquired taste,
No bottoms-up, No spillage in haste.
It doesn't last forever, my friend
You've got to keep it flowing,
Before you hit the bottom,
You've got to pour yourself one another.

28. Finding Love

I once found love,
In a wastepaper bin.
Crumpled and dissed,
And yet, it had a poetic win!
I once found love,
On the windshield of a car.
Nestled in dust, and yet happy…
like a mystic, in a medieval bazaar.
I once found love,
Emblazoned on an empty coffee cup.
Hot pink, garish, and yet…
it made my imagination chin up.
I once found love,
Hidden in a holy book,
Blasphemous, inappropriate,
And yet, it made me repeatedly look.
I once found love,
Drying out on the clothesline.
A long-forgotten gift – wrinkled and damp,
And yet basking in the sunshine!
I once found love,
In a half-eaten, melting chocolate bar,
Sinful, disgusting,

and yet delightfully mysterious,

Like the story of Alexandra and the Russian Tsar.

I once found love,

In 70 missed calls,

Anxious, desperate, a red flag,

And yet, it makes you embrace the fall.

Love is found in the deepest and darkest of trenches,

Crawl into them,

And you will form heart-shaped silhouettes on empty park benches.

Love is found in front of a Howitzer,

Bite the bullet,

And your saga will win a Pulitzer.

Love is found in the horrible soy,

Eat it, and your life will be as beautiful as Helen of Troy

Love is found in the most terrible things,

You've got to bear the brunt,

Before it becomes all the bells, whistles, and rings.

Love is found in the darkest of alleys,

Walk through them,

And Harry will meet Sally.

Finding love is tedious, tough, and dangerous,

You won't find it under your rug,

It's not without reason that they say,

That love is a drug!

29. Great Expectations

If only your smile could rise,
Like the sun in the East,
If only I could bake bread,
Without hating the thought of yeast,
If only I could lull you to sleep,
Without making you weep,
I would be God, no?

30. I Promise

In these troubled times,
let's not forget
that every story of pain ends
with a 'happily ever after.'
Our story will be no different.

Happy Poems

What Dreams Are Made Of

I heard the symphony of birds,

on a stroll under the sunlit sky.

I watched the clear blue skies fade

into the tapestry of a starlit night.

I joined the dots in the heavens above

made fantastical characters out of them.

I let the crickets lull me to sleep.

The next morning, I did all over again!

31. Soul

Where homes are painted
with colours pinched from the wings of butterflies.
Where the days are dipped in the sweetness
borrowed from honeycombs of the giving bees.
where the scent of happiness
turns the roses red with envy...
That is where I want to live.

32. Dewdrops

Freshly chiseled dewdrops,
resting upon the silken leaf
take you back in time,
into the future,
often make time stand still.
If this isn't a miracle,
I don't know what is.

Verse Case Scenario

The oppressors need a spokesperson.

    The oppressed need a poet.

ABOUT:

Prakash Raghupathi writes about routines, dystopia, rebellions, and sometimes, dewdrops and rainbows. His work is merely cathartic and not intended to incite protests. At least not for now. His previous outing, 'The Armchair Anthology', was a collection of quarantine musings on anything and everything that inspired him or failed to do so. He lives in Bengaluru, India, pursuing his decade+ long, award-winning career as a brand storyteller.